WHERE ARE THE HOOVERVILLES?

US HISTORY 5TH GRADE

Children's American History

In this book, we're going to talk about the Hoovervilles during the Great Depression. So, let's get right to it!

An unemployed man standing near his hut in a New York City shanty town during the Great Depression.

The ***"Roaring Twenties"*** were a period of ten years of peace and prosperity for the American people. Despite Prohibition, many people were having a good time and earning enough money to at least survive if not thrive. Even though the flow of alcohol was restricted, the flow of money wasn't.

Couple dancing on the dance floor

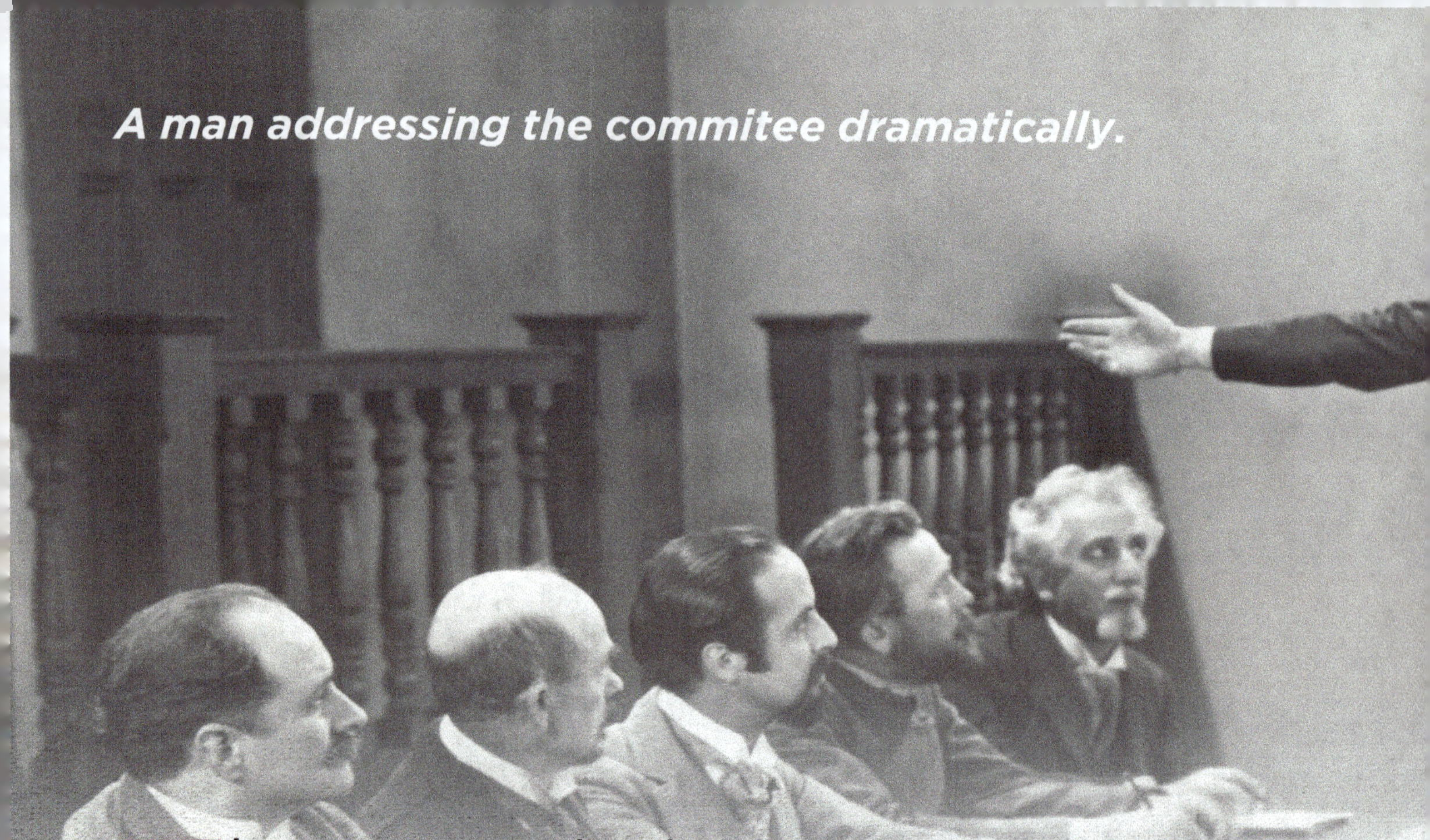

A man addressing the commitee dramatically.

The economy had grown by a factor of more than 6, from 60 to 400 as measured by the Dow Jones Industrial Average. People were investing in stocks in record numbers. Some people had even mortgaged their homes and borrowed money from the stockbrokers in order to buy more stocks. No one thought

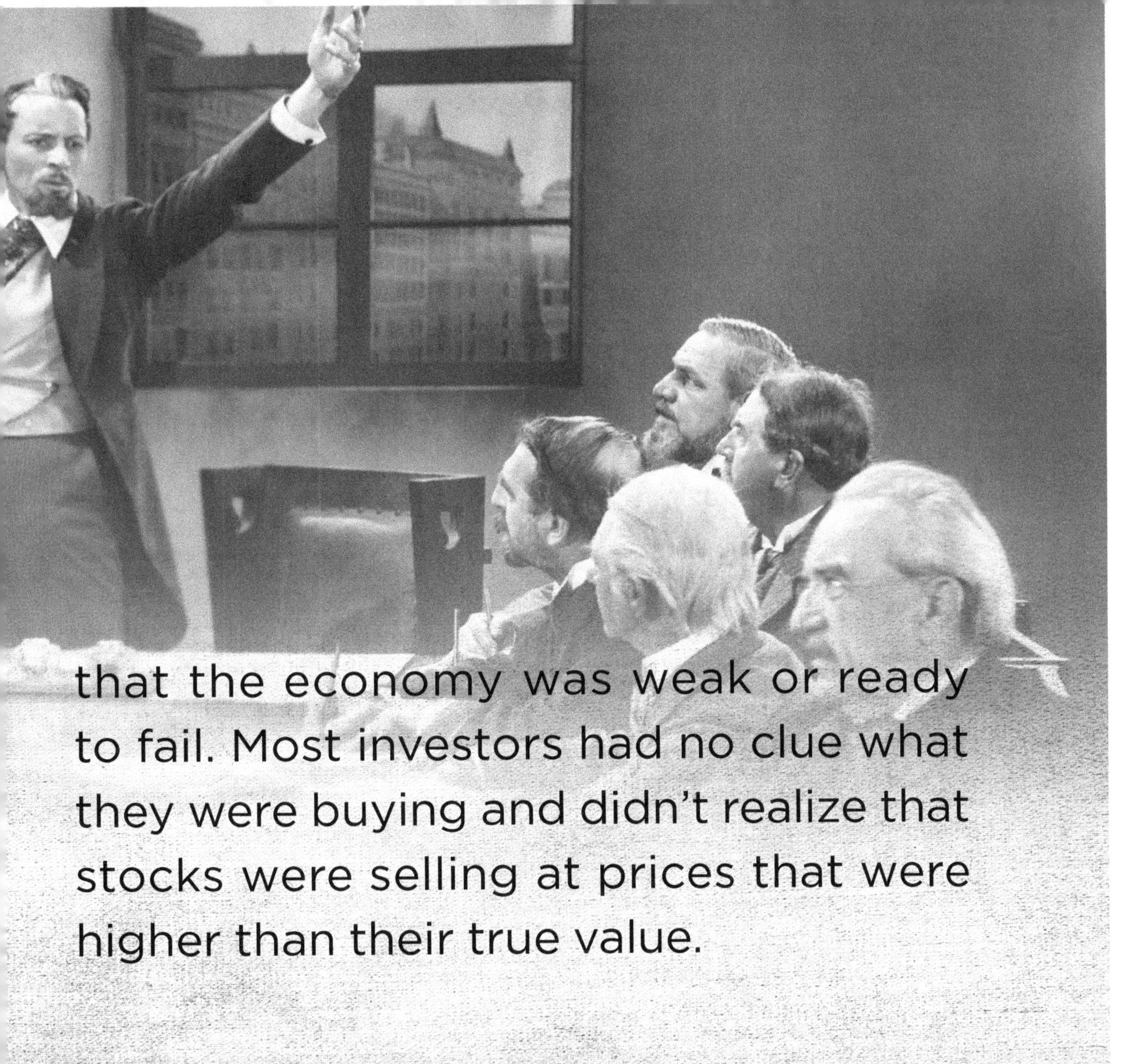

that the economy was weak or ready to fail. Most investors had no clue what they were buying and didn't realize that stocks were selling at prices that were higher than their true value.

President Herbert Hoover was elected in 1928 in a landslide. He had won 40 of the 48 states against the Democratic candidate Al Smith. Hoover took office in 1929 and the economy was slowing a little, but no one thought it was anything to worry about.

Herbert Hoover

Concerned that the stock market was overinflated, Hoover and the Federal Reserve began to raise interest rates. Instead of just slowing a little, stocks began to go down in value quickly. Investors weren't used to this and it made them nervous and nervous investors aren't good for the stock market.

Traders bidding on commodity.

On October 24, 1929, later called Black Thursday, the stock market began a quick decline. By the following Monday and Tuesday, it had crashed. The boom times were over and the Great Depression began.

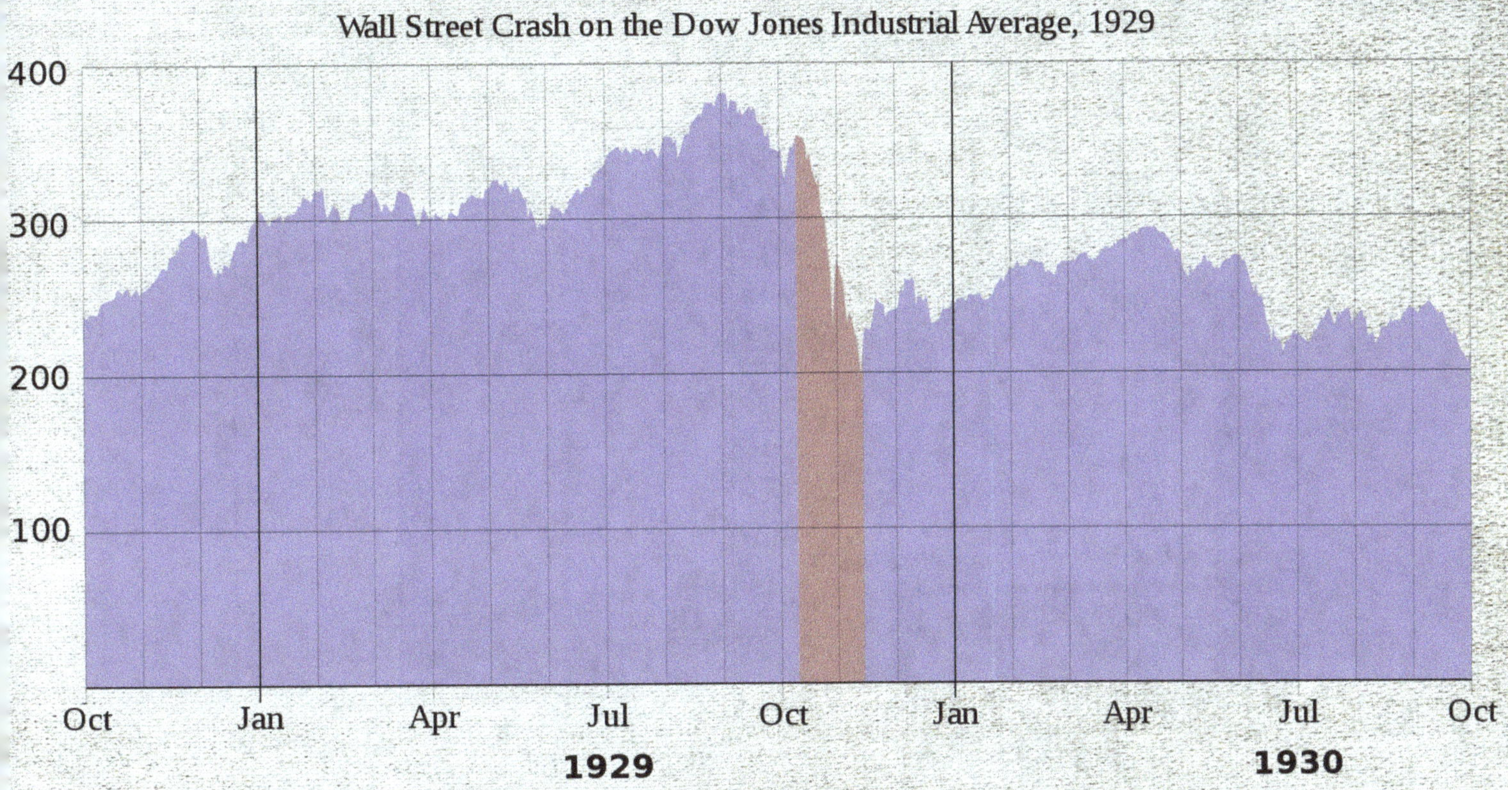

1929 Wall Street crash graph

LINE FOR
1¢ RESTAURANT
20 MEALS FOR $1.
DONATIONS INVITED
HELP FEED THE HUNGRY
I WILL FEED 20
1¢ RESTAURANT
107 W 43rd ST.
D.S.

It took over ten years for the United States to recover from this economic disaster. Many people lost everything that they had. Millionaires became impoverished overnight and were selling apples on the street to make enough to eat. In the cities, men stood in long lines to get a cup of soup so they would have the energy to look for jobs day after day in an economy where jobs were few and far between.

Thousands of banks went bankrupt too because they had taken money from savings deposits and used it to buy stocks so they could make profits. Many families who had never invested in the stock market lost their savings and were wiped out because of the way the banks had handled their money. Many people had such a difficult time emotionally that they ended up committing suicide.

A crowd of depositors protest in the rain at the Bank of United States after its failure.

U.S. GOVERNMENT LIABLE
SAME WAS BANK U.S.
TAX
PAY
NO EVICTIONS
NON PAYMENT RENT
WE WANT
WE DEMAND

Farmer stands in a dust storm in New Mexico, Spring 1935. Photo by Dorothea Lange.

At one point, one third of the people in the United States were living at the poverty level. Even on the farmlands, people were having trouble feeding their families. There had been an intense drought that had turned the topsoil to dust. Huge dust storms were traveling across the plains making it impossible for farmers to grow their crops.

HOOVER WAS BLAMED FOR THE GREAT DEPRESSION

Even though Hoover had tried to sound the alarm about the stock market bubble in both of the presidencies prior to his, no one had listened. Now the country was going through a crisis that wouldn't be easy to fix. Hoover was a Republican and he believed that the federal government shouldn't try to rush in and fix things.

Cartoon of Herbert Hoover as the new President, March 17, 1929. By Oscar Cesare.

UNEMPLOYED
BUY
APPLES
5 EACH

Despite his beliefs, he put some large construction projects on the agenda to get people back to work. He also passed some tax cuts to stimulate the economy. However, the crash and problems that had happened after the crash were too severe and the methods he tried to use were not having a significant effect.

Unemployed man sells apples near the Capitol in Washington D.C.

His lack of a firm grasp on the situation and the reality of how dire things were, was not inspiring confidence in the American people.

Bank failures, increasing unemployment, and bankruptcies of businesses both small and large, were continuing at an alarming pace. The American people now saw him in a completely different way than they had when they had elected him.

Unemployed single women in New York demonstrate for public works jobs.

Association of Unemployed Single Women 22 East 22 St
WE DEMAND JOBS !
PUBLIC WORKS JOBS FOR UNEMPLOYED SINGLE WOMEN !

He wasn't doing anything to save them. A bitter animosity grew toward their president. As many people were forced to leave their homes and became homeless, shanty towns were set up as shelter. They nicknamed these impoverished, run-down, makeshift cities, *"Hoovervilles"* after the president.

Great Depression Hooverville in lower Manhattan. 1932.

It's not clear if the American people came up with the name first, or whether the insult came about because of politics. It is known that the Democratic National Committee's publicity manager, Charles Michelson, used it in an interview. Once the newspapers began using the name to describe the homeless camps, the name was forever associated with Hoover.

An unemployed homeless man stands in the doorway of his rough, but orderly, dwelling in New York's Central Park in 1933.

The Great Depression. A row of out of work men at the New York City docks 1930s.

THE NUMBER OF HOMELESS PEOPLE INCREASES

As the number of homeless people increased, the number of Hoovervilles increased as well. The homeless gathered together, usually near a source of food such as a soup kitchen, to build these makeshift slums. They built shacks from cardboard or wood crates. They tried to hold them together with tar paper or scraps of wood.

Men, women, and children lived in the Hoovervilles. Millions of people lost their money and their jobs during the Great Depression. They couldn't afford their homes anymore and the banks foreclosed on their properties. Sometimes entire families huddled together in a one-room shack that wasn't much sturdier than a cardboard

Poor mother and children, Oklahoma, 1930s by Dorothea Lange.

box. They had been thrown out of their homes and had no place else to go.

BARD

The conditions were horrible and unsanitary in these shanty towns. The shacks were very small and not built well. They didn't have indoor plumbing. During the freezing winters, they offered no warmth and they got wet indoors when it rained. During warm weather, they were stiflingly hot.

A Hooverville near Portland, Oregon.

Huts in West Houston and Mercer St., in Manhattan, 1935.

Because of the lack of running water and restrooms, the conditions were not sanitary. People didn't have clean, sterilized drinking water so they got sick from bacteria, viruses, and other

parasites and their immune systems were compromised. Once someone got sick from a contagious disease, it spread rapidly among everyone living there.

Squatter's shacks in Central Park with the landmark Dakota Apartment building in the background.

HOW BIG WERE THE HOOVERVILLES?

Hoovervilles were all different sizes. Some only had a few hundred people. Others had a thousand people or more. Many of the larger Hoovervilles were in major Metropolitan areas such as New York City and Seattle. The St. Louis Hooverville became so large that it had churches and its own major, who was unofficial.

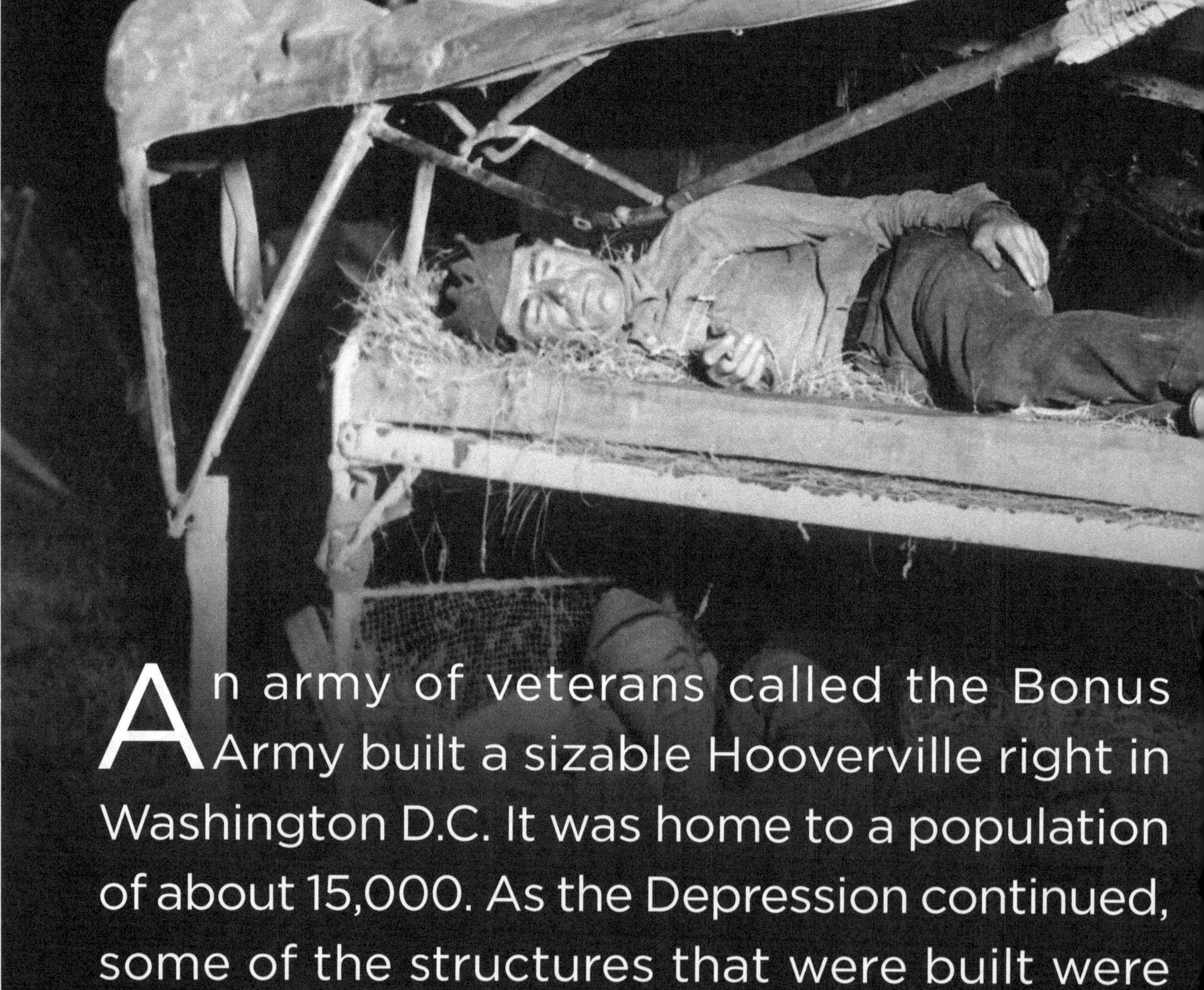

An army of veterans called the Bonus Army built a sizable Hooverville right in Washington D.C. It was home to a population of about 15,000. As the Depression continued, some of the structures that were built were made from more permanent materials such as stone and pieces of wood. However, some

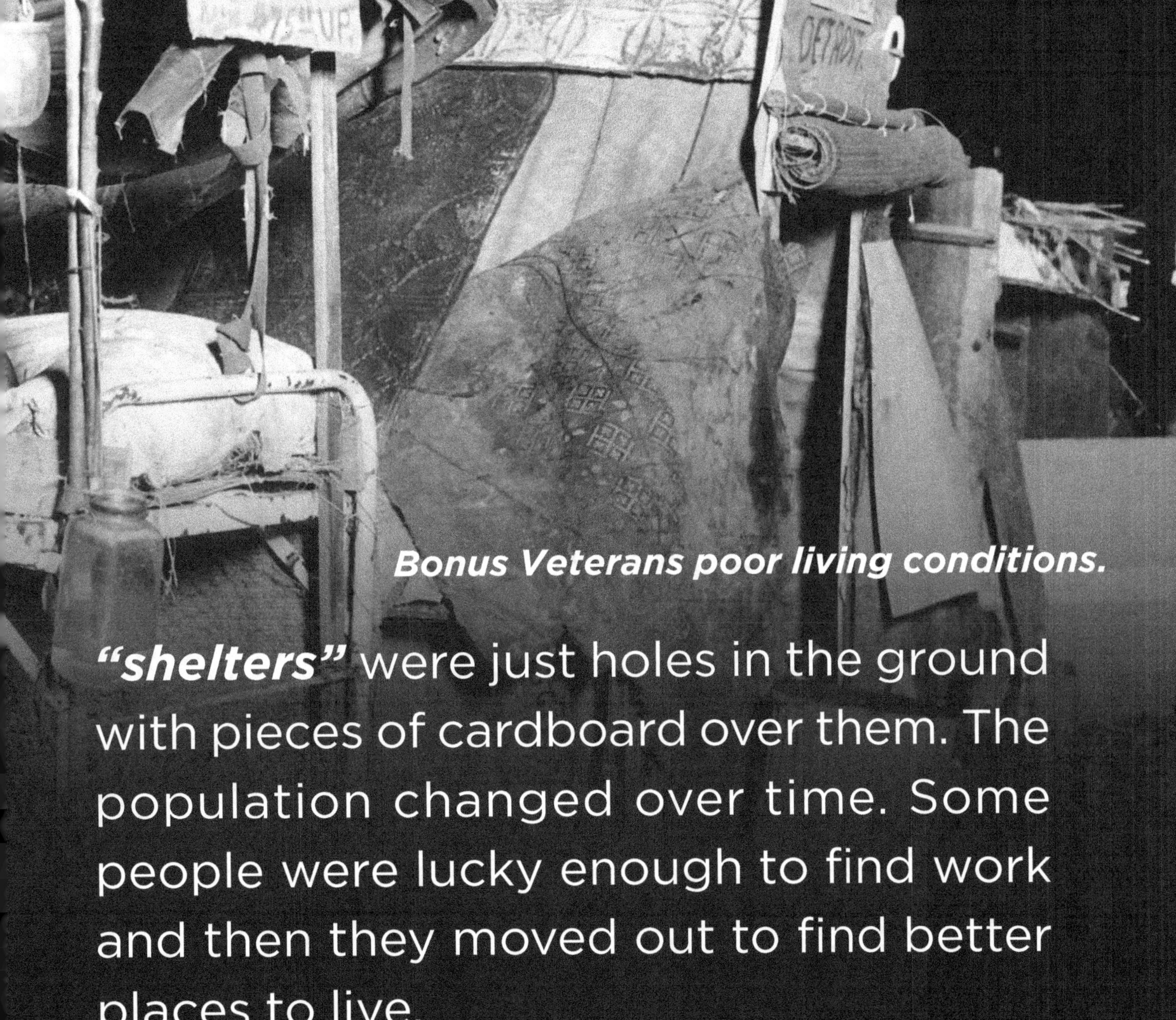

Bonus Veterans poor living conditions.

"*shelters*" were just holes in the ground with pieces of cardboard over them. The population changed over time. Some people were lucky enough to find work and then they moved out to find better places to live.

Tramps traveling in a freight car pass the time playing cards.

TRAVELING HOBOS

Not everyone who was homeless lived in one of the Hoovervilles. Some people were hobos. They jumped on trains and went around the country looking for work. They had symbols they would mark on places that other hobos could see. Their signs were like pictograms that indicated whether people were friendly or not or where they could get a handout and some kind words.

During the Great Depression a man salvages good coal from slag heaps at Nanty Glo, Pennsylvania, for which he is paid ten cents per 100 pounds.

SOUP KITCHENS

At the beginning of the Great Depression, charities ran the soup kitchens. Eventually, the government stepped in to offer soup to the homeless and the unemployed. Soup was cheap and if people were able bodied they would be able to continue to seek work, so it made sense for the government to ensure that people wouldn't starve.

Unemployed men at Volunteers of America Soup Kitchen in Washington D.C.

CROSSING
RAIL ROAD
LOOK OUT FOR THE CARS

Hoovervilles weren't the only things named after President Hoover. People called newspapers ***"Hoover blankets"*** since this is what they used to cover themselves at night in the shanty towns.

Itinerant worker, traveling by foot, looking for work in mines, lumber camps, or farms.

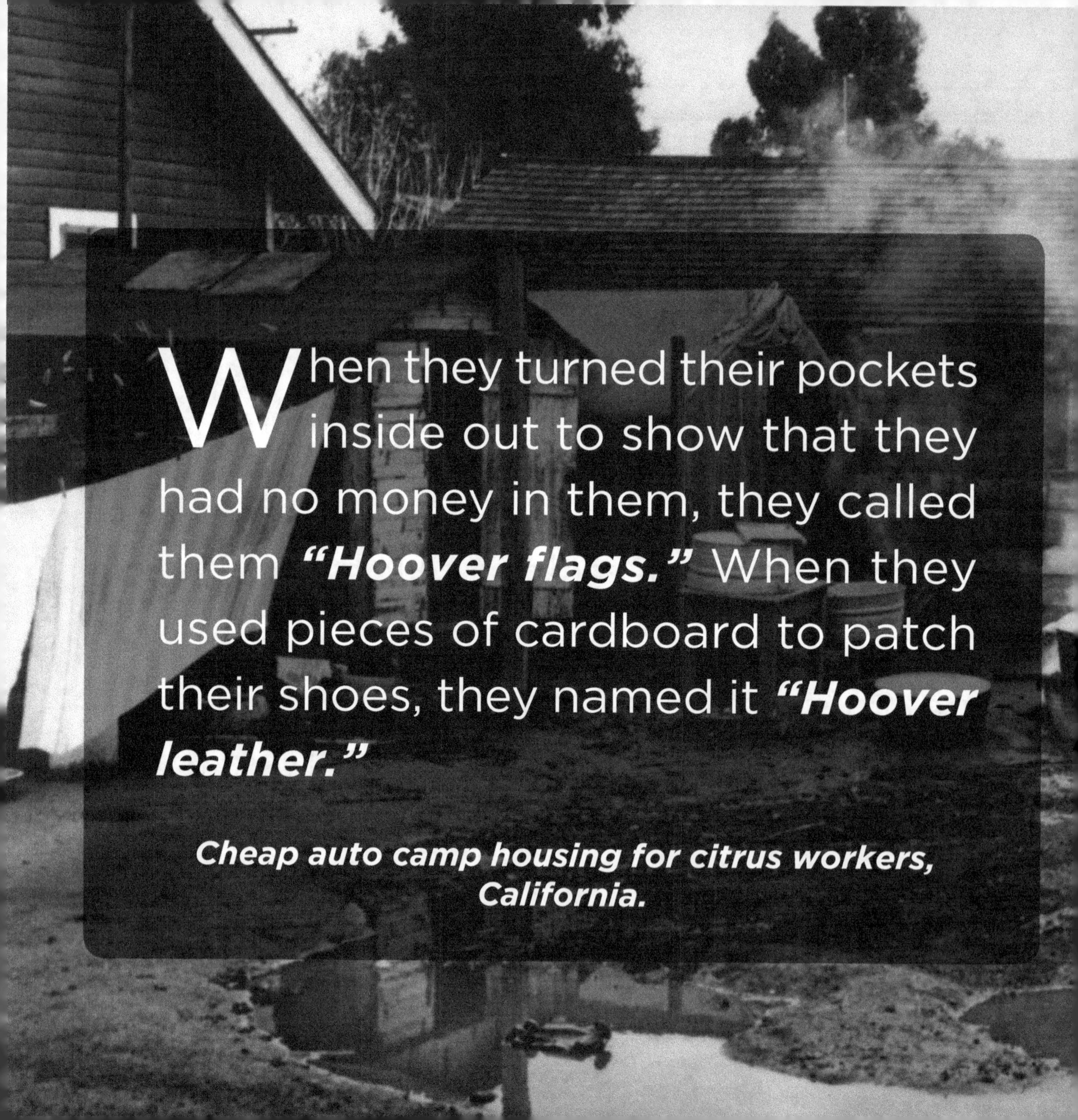

W hen they turned their pockets inside out to show that they had no money in them, they called them **"Hoover flags."** When they used pieces of cardboard to patch their shoes, they named it **"Hoover leather."**

Cheap auto camp housing for citrus workers, California.

THE END OF THE HOOVERVILLES

When the Great Depression finally ended, people started to leave the Hoovervilles in larger numbers. By the year 1941, the government put programs into place so that these impoverished shanty towns would be removed from the landscape.

Ex-tenant farmer on relief grant in the Imperial Valley, California.

THE ELECTION OF 1932

After Hoover had been the president for one term, it was time for another election. The American people were ready for a change. The Democratic candidate Franklin D. Roosevelt promised changes that would yield an economic recovery.

A Nebraska farmer meets with a Farm Security Administration Debt Adjustment Committee for help to avoid foreclosure of his farm mortgage. May 1936

They were looking for the *"savior"* who could fix the hardships that they had experienced since the end of 1929. During his campaign, Hoover said something to the effect that ***"things could be worse."*** He had completely lost the trust of the American people. Roosevelt won by a landslide and proceeded to put programs in place to get the country back to work.

Unemployed men filling out Social Security benefit claims, ca. 1938.

Now you know more about the Hoovervilles. You can find more American History books from Baby Professor by searching the website of your favorite book retailer.

'Oakies' couple migrating.

Visit
BABY PROFESSOR
EDUCATION KIDS
www.BabyProfessorBooks.com
to download Free Baby Professor eBooks
and view our catalog of new and exciting
Children's Books

www.ingramcontent.com/pod-product-compliance
Lightning Source LLC
Chambersburg PA
CBHW080806120726
48001CB00009B/2863